Incomplete

A Poetry Collection

Rawad Shaban
Faezah

Incomplete
Copyright © 2020 by Rawad Shaban and Faezah

All rights reserved. No part of this publication may be reproduced, distributed, or transmitted in any form or by any means, including photocopying, recording, or other electronic or mechanical methods, without the prior written permission of the author, except in the case of brief quotations embodied in critical reviews and certain other non-commercial uses permitted by copyright law.

Tellwell Talent
www.tellwell.ca

ISBN
978-0-2288-2540-1 (Paperback)

The Guts

PART 1
First Flame
1

PART 2
Sorrow
31

PART 3
Melancholic Rain
89

Thank You's

Thank you, O, for being the spark
Thank you, M, for showing me my art
Thank you, E, for giving me the Emotion
Thank you, Friends, for all the support
Thank you, Family, for everything
Thank you, World, for listening to my heart pulse

Illustrations by Faezah
Instagram: @Imfaezah

Part 1

First Flame

Her light
As bright as the moon
She rocks me like a wave
As I crash against her sands
Giving and taking

We are a puzzle with all the pieces
No complications
Hand in hand
We are the lock with two keys
On the bridge of memories
Floating in the wind

Our bodies like pieces
    Completing each other's puzzle
    Picture perfect

Forces of attraction
The invisible laws of (e)motion
Pushing and pulling
Rooting and drifting
Positives and negatives
That make (e)motion

The sun rays are no match
For your radiance
Your golden shine
And all its healing powers

Yellow princess

The waves crash
    Moving for the moon
        The ocean laps the earth
            And It's all thanks to you

You came like the wind to my ambers
Igniting my heart once more
The ink spilling
No control
No satisfaction
Just the pulsing beat
The steady Rhythm of you through me

These blank pages give me headaches so I fill them up with my feelings and when I can't I close my eyes and think about the past but lately my eyes don't close and these pages are never empty because the thoughts that I let myself think and the feelings I let myself feel about you could fill books. You fill me up with hope for the future and my mind wanders and I could never show you my book of thoughts because you wouldn't understand it. I hate you sometimes because you do stupid things but I love you most of the time because you deserve to be loved and I want to give you everything. You feed My hungry butterflies.

Shades
Of all colours
Mellow yellow on the sun
Cool blue calms the ocean
Pastel pink in the sky
And in your eyes
Shades
Of my heart

Euphoria talks
It whispers goosebumps
And shouts from the heavens
It finds home
In the darkest of minds

It sings
Notes of sweetness
Like butterflies migrating around your body

From your head forming thoughts
To your lungs breathing out words
To your stomach giving you feelings

Euphoria exists
In the eye of your mind

Your eyes smile
The most beautiful smile
Words need not be spoken
Only passed through movement
Gestures of you

The blue of you
As blue as a violet
As churning
As brash
As opaque
As smooth as the sky
You are an ultraviolet incandescence
In a world of boring colours

You are the weakness and I
Fall every time

You are beautiful in my eye
You are divine

I will be the shoulder
I will be the wall
I will be the rock
The anchor and the ground
                        Rest on me
                        Stability
                        Rest on me
                        Indefinitely

Move me like you do
Make the shadows
That follow you
Stand me with them
Sit me down
Dance with me
Behind you

You're a bright star
In my world of darkness
Light the way and flood my eyes
For I have been way too ignorant
Bitter taste I grind my teeth
With haste I swallow my pride
For you are not mine yet
But give me time
I Put my heart on my sleeve
And pray you don't break it
For I am yours and you are mine
Life is short
There is No time

She is not your full moon but the crescent on a summer night
Shimmering in its beauty
Incomplete yet perfect
A metaphor of its own

For you
What I wouldn't do
All the things
For the thought of you

The heart grows
    Pulsing into new vessels
        Red crowds the room
            And love is in the air

The pond rippled waves filled with the reflection of blurred happiness.
Life
Was
Simple.

Part 2

Sorrow

Need you now
More than ever
I'm missing
I'm lost
Just like all my sweaters

Your ever-radiating warmth
A wave of comfort with no end
The walls are closing in
And I am cold again

The moon lit up our dark rooms

And our hearts spilled ink

Marking paper

To never be taken back

Goodbye for a little while
My dear love
How I will miss you
And the grain of your face
Your fingers painted the world
In a different colour
And without your touch
I am blinded

Honesty

So lost in the days that we forget all about it
Words promised
Actions forgotten

Fake short-lived bliss

The clouds don't dance
Not like they used to
              The rain drops fall harder
              On the bleak world
The sun doesn't smile
Not like it used to

Error: *143*
Emotionally unavailable
Try again later

Lately I've been running on fumes

Puffs of life

Exhaustion takes the throne

And the cycle resets

Your mind is hardened clay
And my hands are tired

Easily forgotten
Is how I'll be remembered

Thoughts and feelings
With little resemblance

Blurs in history

Words
Flow out of your mouth
With manipulative intent
Oppressive behavior
Anger
Fills the veins
And I am drained

It is quiet on your side of the bed
The walls don't move anymore
Life is fading
And I am a white flag swaying

It never was subtle
Instant and abrupt
A rock skipping the water
When will it sink?

It sailed quickly
The yellow boat
And it was lost again
In the distance
behind the sun

Your waters rock the boat
      Whooshing
           Crashing
Nothing ahead
Nothing behind
A desert of salt
I am seasick

You built yourself up with paragraphs
You filled books
And now I see
they are stories
made of broken promises

Too much of you
Is Never enough

I was full
But you left me empty

The shallow heart
Drowns in the deep
          Gasping for breath
          Living off defeat
Survivor of the pain
Stop all your anger
          Take a step back
          And leave that stranger
And watch what your breath does
when you breathe fire
          The world is Smothered
          Sit back and admire

I can see through you
I can see in you
I see the hole left
Love once taken from you

        An empty space
        An empty heart
        Drink drink drink
        We fall apart

Cold and hot
Is how you are
No reason
No excuse
Close or far

I drained my heart
For now it does not pump

There is no colour
There is no blood

Love me as I am
And maybe I will live

To give you back the blood
You wish to give

The red never passes
It bursts and subsides
It screams and whispers
Built into the roots
That drain the soul

The Line part 1

Walk the line
The line of life
Walk it straight
And never look back
Let it guide you
Until the end
And now
You are lost

The Line part 2

My eyes stare straight
I walk the line
Blinders on
Rushing for time
But the harder I stare
The longer it takes
Because I can't look left
I can't look right
My blinders are on
I have no sight

I float
In circles I go
Looping the infinite
For infinity

        My days are marked
        Yet I have not stopped
        Looping the infinite
        For all of eternity

As we sinned all night and the sun came up
our lives were tangled in a mess of yarn in
which we used to sow our broken hearts

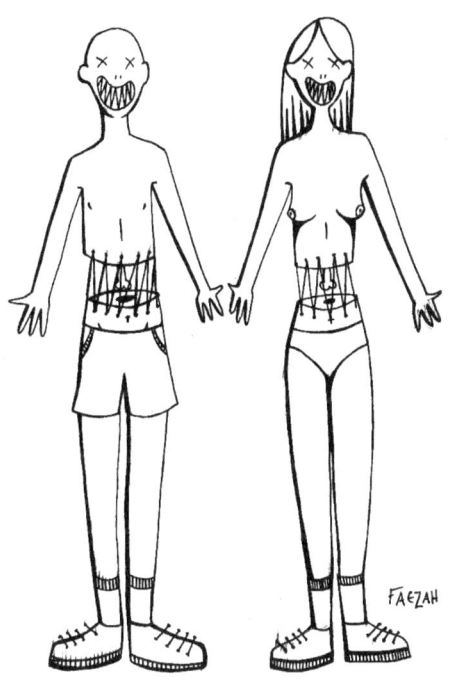

The vacant mind
    Leaves no room
Leaves no stone
    Left unturned

Every story
    Played until the end
Every scenario
    Played out in my head

The days move slow
But the weeks move fast
Time cannot stay
But time cannot pass
I am stuck in days of old
But I am living the days of new
The mind is trapped

But it is free of you

A grain of sand
Is all it takes
A little bit of love
And you fall

Do you hear it in my voice?
    The quake
    The rasp

Can you feel it in my heart?
    The thump
    The pound

Do you see it in my eyes?
    The shadows
    The drain

And you say I don't love you?

I am lost
Until I am found
Inside my dreams
That I will forget in the morning
Goodnight

You are cold
A frozen pond
Shining slippery
Reflecting the image of me
Yet it is blurred
With scratches and patches
Colourless
Confusing
Creation

Forever is a day of the week
Or a year of a century
Forever and ever
Never forget
Forever is not real

Am I not worth your love?
Am I a pawn in your game?
Am I special?
Am I real?

I cry for all I am
Is what you have made me
A pebble in the creek
Drowning in your waters
Forming in your current
Swimming in your waves
Every night

The poison that you were
Feels clear like water
I gulp my last gulp
Fall to my knees
And pray
For the devil is here

The morning sun smiles
On the leaves wet from last night's tears
The morning dew
The blue now gold
Fantastically ecstatic for the new day
The morning is due

My wild thought
Is with you

I am irrational
In my mind

I am a hole
In your heart

Another cigarette
It won't hurt
Feeling numb to the damage
The rush of death
The delay of life

You are noise
With no sound
Eating me alive
With no way out

        Ask me how I feel
        All you'll hear is the noise
        All I feel
        All I am

    Is the sound of you

You are the sum of my present
And the difference of my past
You are the eye of the storm
In the storm of my mind

You erupt
Spilling the waves of you on all who would have it
Drowning the truth
Sinking love
Deep in your murky waters of deception

No sight
Blinders of anger
And sadness

You fill the gap in my life
But you are nothing more
And that is more dangerous than any other form of love
Because it is not love
It is deception out of convenience
It is a sadistic satire
That has no purpose but humiliation

It knocks at the door
    Open
    And love
    And heartache
    And desire
    And disaster
    And close

And then it knocks again

My memory is blurred like a fog
I remember you being so peaceful
So solid
So tangible
And then suddenly
You were gone
Slipped from my arms and disappeared
It stung
But it doesn't sting anymore
It aches
And not because you left
But because you took a part of me with you

back to the same page
Back to the sadness
Back to the pit
How do I fix this
How do I move on
How do I love again

My veins
     Drained
My mind
     blank
My soul
     black
My end
     Near

The innocence on the ground
Like spilled water you run
The stream of sadness you control
Let my tears drop
Let my heart ache
For I do not deserve your oceans

As the night climbed to its peak
The moon was live
All I could see was the Darkness in which I am engulfed by
The stream of sadness that has swept my heart
And drowned my soul
Now I stand a bottle full of pain
Let my ache be
And my mind rest

The shadows of the sea show me faces of hopelessness
Tears of salt that remind me of you
The cuts will heal
But the scars will stay
A living reminder of the affliction

Part 3
Melancholic Rain

I dreamt a dream
Of love and peace
Of eyes that glimmer
Of lips that tease
        The minds that meet
        In dreams at last
        Are Lovers of distance
        Or Lovers of past
I cherished the kiss
For it was a memory
I dreamt of the bliss
She did not give to me
        Our story did end
        Now a new beginning
        I love you my love
        But our light is dimming

I am sprinting
Lungs at capacity
And I still breathe
I glide through the air
Moving with the wind
My heart pumps with every step
Adrenaline buzzing
Euphoric

There are drawings in the clouds that paint a picture only I can see and they say I am a free bird

Paint the sky red and let me live
    For I am the heart and soul of a true colour

As I reflect on what once was
I remember what has become
And wonder what will be

Of me

Shimmering water
Somber fellow
The dock is long
And the night is short

Better days
To come
To be

Better days
Have come
Are here

The leaves will sprout again
Things will change
That is the circle of life

There you were once more waiting for me
Again and again
But I'm afraid you're on the other side of the river
And I cannot cross the bridge you burnt

As blind as love can be, we can be blinder
Our lives are spent hiding and shying away from
Opportunities that can change our lives forever
Take a chance
Take a risk
Step up
Let the waves of life hit and do your best to stay
Above water
Because that's what we do
We survive
Even with bricks tied to our feet
Even with chains around our souls
We survive
Life means nothing to death
So why does death mean everything to life?

The sand is just grain without the ocean

The scars are just pain without the lessons

The world is just lonely without the people we love

Goodbye

As you came I became delirious
A sudden state of euphoria
Softly humming to myself the tune of you
Rushing through my veins an almost neon taste
Teasing my mind, body, and soul with the thought of happiness
As your head laid against my shoulder, my life felt with purpose
You were like me
Lost waiting to be found
But not wanting to be found
We had found each other
My heart lured by soft kisses and a connection
Only to be trapped in "love"
A dangerous game to play but I gamble
And I lose
My eyes opened
And my mind began plunging into the darkness
An all-consuming desire that could never be fulfilled
It was not as it seemed
Happiness is not eternal

And one can only live for the memories
For what are we if not our memories
Time does not stop
Life does not stop
Desire does not stop
So lust
Live
Move on
And never limit yourself for you never know what is instore

Our chapter ends
A new chapter begins
For me
For you
In a different book

Let her be
    As she is
        No change

You can never expect change
You can only hope for it

Hope cannot dictate your decisions

Time is relative
Life is imaginary
Use your imagination

From lovers to strangers
It's the cycle
It's the life of lovers

When the clouds of despair are at your door
And your head is low
Stand straight in the face of scrutiny
And March on

A message
To he who listens
To she who thinks
To they who do not lie
Open your eyes

And see

I have lost
But I am here
Moving like a flower
The petals forced out of me
The seeds by the water
Plant me deep
Put me in the dark
Parch me until I crack
And yet I grow
I will find the sun

Incomplete
Growing with every experience
We can never be empty

Only half full

Interaction
It's all about control
How we use it
How we give it
How we take it

Causing us to live vicariously through others
Like toys

Playing and pushing and wearing and tearing
Until collapse

Ruins

These lines I write
Like drugs
My soul is addicted to the freedom
The aura
The vibe
Of the social circus

Take me back to the days of bliss
The nights of no end
And the hearts of warmth
Summer

If you love yourself you'll listen
You'll take care and forget
You'll move on and heal
You'll live you'll love and you won't let it get you down
Because your strength is greater than your weakness
There will always be bad times
So enjoy the good while you can

Don't run
They wouldn't leap
Don't walk
They wouldn't crawl
Don't chase
They will never change

You wish to waltz
The waltz of me
My dance is dazing
Dazzling your feet
The moves you make
Marking the sand
Twisting and turning
Teaching the land
The motion of emotion

You ought not say
It'll be okay
For when life does not
It will not give way

With him
Or her
Or them saying you'll be okay

The sun will not shine
Until the rain goes away

I am Lost
But found is where I'll be
In a year
Or 5
Or 10 or 20

Gasps of breath
Shock and excitement
Serotonin rushes and I am alive again
One step at a time

Empty letters
Empty words
Empty people
But the glass is still half full

The moment

A second of your life slowed down to bits
The puzzle pieces are beautiful
But were never complete
The moment becomes memory
And the memory is lost

Note to self
You are who you make yourself
You are your decisions
Never doubt yourself
For living in the moment should be temporary
And you will never surrender to regret

There will be times you will forget
Times you will be happy
For a moment
Or for an eternity
No matter how sad the world seems
There is no happiness without sadness

Your journey is long
And your shoes are too small
Your laces are untied
And your soles are beaten
The colour is fading
And the fabric is torn
Excuses I gave
Not to walk your mile

The land is long
Yellow and calm
The wind slight
And the road empty
Driving with no destination
The journey of self-discovery

Look at the colours
    Red yellow blue
Listen to the birds
    That chirp for you
Orange is the sky
    Beautiful shades
Blue is the water
    The sky never fades

Bland mornings
With dull afternoons
Repeating evenings
That lead to true colours in the night
The process that never stops
The colours that keep me living

The changes we make to ourselves matter
The edges that are rough
And the edges that are smooth
Picking and scraping at every detail makes us
Us
The importance of growth

When the time is right
We'll be happy
When the time is right
We'll really live
When the time is right

It's already too late

We grow
Into new
Out of old
Change without growth
Is downfall
Growth without change
Does not exist

Change is not the enemy
It is your friend
Change is growth
And Growth is power

Hey there princess
Don't you cry
Things will be okay
From time to time
Life isn't always perfect
There's ups and there's downs
Enjoy the rollercoaster
While you're still around

It's strange
What we are
    Enjoying the present
    With no means to a future
Forming a relationship
With no attachment

The art of us

If love was a poem
It wouldn't be happy
It wouldn't be sad
It wouldn't be sappy

        If love was a poem
        It wouldn't be words
        It wouldn't be letters
        It wouldn't be verbs

If love was a poem
It would not be real
For love is the mind
Love is how we feel

Feed your desires
    And tame your beast
Let it take you
    Down the path of self control

Atop the white cloud we floated
Higher than the mountains and the trees

        The pressure so strong
        The oxygen so little
        It's getting harder to breathe

It's time to fall from the top to the bottom
And stand up taller than ever

        Chin up
        Chest out

Soon you'll never have been better

The mind
I cannot find
Is the mind of truth
That of love
And affection
The mind of openness
And forgiveness
That shatters into a million pieces
Yet
Is together

Thank you me
Thank you for all you've done
Thank you for always loving me
And respecting me
Thank you for not forgetting me
Or abandoning me
Thank you for existing

To conclude, there is no conclusion. This book is unfinished and never will be in my mind of minds. The same is not necessarily said about yours. Find your path. Follow it and never stop tryi-

www.ingramcontent.com/pod-product-compliance
Lightning Source LLC
LaVergne TN
LVHW011837060526
838200LV00053B/4079